Strategic Studies Institute
and
U.S. Army War College Press

LEGALITY IN CYBERSPACE:
AN ADVERSARY VIEW

Keir Giles
with
Andrew Monaghan

March 2014

*****

Comments pertaining to this report are invited and should be forwarded to: Director, Strategic Studies Institute and U.S. Army War College Press, U.S. Army War College, 47 Ashburn Drive, Carlisle, PA 17013-5010.

*****

This manuscript was funded by the U.S. Army War College External Research Associates Program. Information on this program is available on our website, *www.StrategicStudies Institute.army.mil*, at the Opportunities tab.

*****

The Strategic Studies Institute and U.S. Army War College Press publishes a monthly email newsletter to update the national security community on the research of our analysts, recent and forthcoming publications, and upcoming conferences sponsored by the Institute. Each newsletter also provides a strategic commentary by one of our research analysts. If you are interested in receiving this newsletter, please subscribe on the SSI website at *www.StrategicStudiesInstitute.army.mil/newsletter*.

FOREWORD

While conflict in cyberspace is not a new phenomenon, the legality of hostile cyber activity at a state level remains imperfectly defined. While there is broad agreement among the United States and its allies that cyber warfare would be governed by existing law of armed conflict, with no need for additional treaties or conventions to regulate hostilities online, this view is not shared by many nations that the United States could potentially face as adversaries.

A range of foreign states use definitions for cyber conflict that are entirely different from our own, extending to different concepts of what constitutes online hostilities and even a state of war. This leads to a potentially dangerous situation where an adversary could be operating according to an entirely different understanding of international law to that followed by the United States.

In this Letort Paper, Mr. Keir Giles uses Russian-language sources and interviews to illustrate the very distinct set of views on the nature of conflict in cyberspace that pertains to Russia. He provides an important window into Russian thinking and explains how fundamental Russian assumptions on the nature of cyber activity need to be considered when countering, or engaging with, Russian cyber initiatives.

The Strategic Studies Institute is pleased to offer this detailed analysis as an essential guide to the mindset of an important cyber actor, and one which it is essential for the United States to understand.

DOUGLAS C. LOVELACE, JR.
Director
Strategic Studies Institute and
   U.S. Army War College Press

ABOUT THE AUTHORS

KEIR GILES is the director of the Conflict Studies Research Centre (CSRC), a group of deep subject matter experts on Eurasian security formerly attached to the United Kingdom (UK) Ministry of Defence. Now operating in the private sector, CSRC provides in-depth analysis on security issues affecting Russia and its relations with overseas partners. After beginning his career working with paramilitary aviation in the former Soviet Union and Ukraine immediately following the fall of the Soviet Union, Mr. Giles joined the BBC Monitoring Service (BBCM) to report on political and military affairs in the former Soviet space. While attached from BBCM to CSRC at the UK Defence Academy, he wrote and briefed for UK and North Atlantic Treaty Organization (NATO) government agencies on Russian defense and security issues. Uniquely, he is a double Associate Fellow of the Royal Institute of International Affairs (Chatham House) in London, UK, as well as a regular contributor to research projects on Russian security issues in both the UK and Europe. Mr. Giles's work has appeared in academic and military publications across Europe and in the United States.

ANDREW MONAGHAN is a Research Fellow in the Russia and Eurasia Programme at Chatham House and Academic Visitor at St Antony's College, Oxford, UK. Additionally, he is the Founder and Director of the Russia Research Network, an independent organization for the generation of information and expertise on Russian politics, security, and economic issues based in London. In this capacity, he has served as an expert witness to the House of Commons Foreign Affairs Select Committee. Until late 2012, Dr. Monaghan directed Russia related research in the Research Division of the NATO Defense College in Rome. In this role, he was also the senior researcher on energy security matters. Prior to that, he held positions as a Senior Research Associate at the Advanced Research and Assessment Group, part of the Defence Academy of the UK, and a Visiting Lecturer in the Defence Studies Department of King's College, London, the civilian academic arm of the Joint Services Command and Staff College at the Defence Academy. Dr. Monaghan holds an M.A. in war studies and a Ph.D. in Russian foreign policy (Russian perspectives of Russia-European Union security relations) from the Department of War Studies, King's College.

SUMMARY

The United States and its allies are in general agreement on the legal status of conflict in cyberspace. Although key principles remain unresolved, such as what precisely constitutes an armed attack or use of force in cyberspace, overall there is a broad legal consensus among Euro-Atlantic nations that existing international law and international commitments are sufficient to regulate cyber conflict.

This principle is described in multiple authoritative legal commentaries. But these can imply misleadingly that this consensus is global and unchallenged. In fact, China, Russia, and a number of like-minded nations have an entirely different concept of the applicability of international law to cyberspace as a whole, including to the nature of conflict within it. These nations could therefore potentially operate in cyberspace according to entirely different understandings of what is permissible under international humanitarian law, the law of armed conflict, and other legal baskets governing conduct during hostilities.

U.S. policymakers cannot afford to underestimate the extent to which Russian concepts and approaches differ from what they may take for granted. This includes the specific question of when, or whether, hostile action in cyberspace constitutes an act or state of war. Recent Russian academic and military commentary stresses the blurring of the distinction between war and peace, and asks to what extent this distinction still exists. This suggestion of a shifting boundary between war and peace is directly relevant to consideration of at what point Russia considers itself to be at war and therefore subject to specific legal constraints on actions in cyberspace.

Conversely, actions that are considered innocent and friendly by the United States and European nations are parsed as hostile actions by Russia, leading to Russian attempts to outlaw "interference in another state's information space." The Russian notion of what constitutes a cyber weapon—or in Russian terminology, an information weapon—is radically different from our assumptions.

Initiatives put forward by Russia for international cooperation on legal initiatives governing cyber activity have received a mixed response from other states. But they need to be taken into account because of the alternative consensus on cyber security opposing the views of the United States and its close allies, which is growing as a result of an effective Russian program of ticking up support for Moscow's proposals from other countries around the world.

This Letort Paper explores the Russian approach to legal constraints governing actions in cyberspace within the broader framework of the Russian understanding of the nature of international law and commitments, with the aim of informing U.S. military and civilian policymakers of views held by a potential adversary in cyberspace. Using a Russian perspective to examine the legal status of various activities in cyberspace, including what constitutes hostile activity, demonstrates that assumptions commonly held in the United States may need to be adjusted to counter effectively—or engage with—Russian cyber initiatives.

LEGALITY IN CYBERSPACE:
AN ADVERSARY VIEW

INTRODUCTION

The United States and its allies devote considerable time and expense to considering the legal dimensions of cyber conflict. Although key definitions for establishing legality remain unresolved, such as what precisely constitutes an armed attack or use of force in cyberspace, the legal debates within and between Euro-Atlantic militaries are generally in harmony and derive from a broader legal consensus in these nations. This consensus holds that existing international law and international commitments are sufficient to regulate cyber conflict, and furthermore that certain individual rights in using cyberspace are inalienable.

Authoritative legal commentaries, such as the *Tallinn Manual on the International Law Applicable to Cyber Warfare*, released in early 2013,[1] reflect this Western consensus. But they can misleadingly imply that this consensus is global and unchallenged. Significantly, the Manual does not include among its contributors any legal experts from nations considered potential adversaries in cyberspace, notably China and Russia.

In fact, China, Russia, and a number of like-minded nations have an entirely different concept of the applicability of international law to cyberspace as a whole, including to the nature of conflict within it. These nations could therefore potentially operate in cyberspace according to entirely different understandings of what is permissible under international humanitarian law, the law of armed conflict, and other legal baskets governing conduct during hostilities.

1

This Letort Paper will explore the Russian approach to legal constraints governing actions in cyberspace, within the broader framework of the Russian understanding of the nature of international law and commitments, to inform U.S. military and civilian policymakers of views held by a potential adversary in cyberspace. It will examine the legal status of activities in cyberspace, including what constitutes hostile activity from a Russian perspective, to demonstrate that assumptions commonly held in the United States may need to be adjusted effectively to counter—or engage with—Russian cyber initiatives.

THE CYBER SECURITY SCHISM

In conventional conflict, the legal constraints on combatants are clearly understood and well defined. Precisely when and how a state of war arises (*jus ad bellum*) and how parties must conduct themselves during conflict (*jus in bello*) have been established through customary law and international legal commitments over the course of centuries. Generally accepted among developed nations, these principles give a degree of stability and predictability to the extent of armed conflict, particularly in terms of legal constraints on collateral damage, proportionality, initiation of conflict, self-defense, and humanitarian impact.

In cyberspace, no such consensus exists. This is because the view of legality held by the United States and its allies is not a global one, and other key actors in cyberspace have an entirely different approach. It is therefore important for U.S. planners to understand that potential adversaries may be operating according to an entirely different set of assumptions regarding what is permissible behavior in cyberspace in terms of international law.

Descriptions of the state of regulation of activity in cyberspace as a whole are replete with metaphor. Establishing commonly agreed norms and rules of behavior for this new domain has been compared to the early days of nuclear weapons with no mutual understanding on the rules of deterrence, to the motor car with no rules of the road, to the long development of international maritime law, and much else besides. A common perception is that online activity, and in particular hostile online activity, is so new a phenomenon that there should be little surprise that a commonly agreed regulatory framework is still a distant prospect.

Despite the recent burgeoning of domestic and international legal debate over cyber issues, this perception of novelty is misplaced. Neither cyber conflict, nor the legal arguments over it, can remotely be described as a new concept. Among newcomers to cyber issues, it is commonly believed that the notion of introducing hostile code custom written by national-level experts into a secure facility on removable media in order to carry out a precisely targeted attack on a system through a supervisory control and data acquisition (SCADA) interface is an entirely new and original idea never heard of before Stuxnet. Until, that is, they see the original British version of *The Italian Job*, where exactly the same process is described in a motion picture released almost 40 years earlier. As stated by Jason Healey in his survey, "A Fierce Domain," which should be essential reading for anybody who believes that this is a new issue:

Many of the questions vexing cyber policymakers today were asked in exactly the same terms by their predecessors 10 and 20 years earlier. Again and again, lessons have been identified and forgotten rather than learned.[2]

Nevertheless, despite a Euro-Atlantic consensus on the broad principles of cyber conflict and use of the Internet, intense debate between legal practitioners continues, with a marked increase in intensity following the recent prioritization of cyber issues in the United States and the United Kingdom (UK), and associated funding flows. Examples of recent legal scholarship published in the last 12 months alone include "Legal Implications of Territorial Sovereignty in Cyberspace" and "Law of Neutrality in Cyberspace" by leading German specialist Wolff Heintschel Von Heinegg; "A Methodology for Cyber Operations Targeting and Control of Collateral Damage in the Context of Lawful Armed Conflict" by Robert Fanelli; studies examining the applicability of international law to terrorist acts committed through cyberspace;[3] and many more.

Yet all these works, as well as the *Tallinn Manual* referred to previously, reflect only a portion of the global debate over potential cyber law. Studying Russian scholarship on "information warfare" (IW) and international agreements promoted by Russia with varying degrees of success provides an entirely different view. Examination of the Shanghai Cooperation Organization (SCO) Information Security Treaty of 2009, or the draft International Code of Conduct in Cyberspace proposed in the United Nations (UN) jointly by Russia, China, Tajikistan, and Uzbekistan in 2011, illustrates that different nations hold views divergent from those of the United States.

4

One key area of disagreement is whether online activity, and especially online conflict, is broadly governed by existing international law, or whether entirely new legal instruments are needed to govern it. An objective assessment by two authoritative officers of the Organization for Cooperation and Security in Europe (OSCE) notes that "no universally accepted legal framework for dealing with cyber threats exists."[4] This leads Russia, China, and others to call for what Hamadoun Touré, head of the International Telecommunication Union (ITU) has described as:

> a treaty in which countries would promise to ensure Internet access for their citizens, protect them from attacks, work with other countries to stop criminal activities, and not attack another country first.[5]

The United States, by contrast, argues that no such new document is necessary. The result is what German academic and practitioner Sandro Gaycken refers to as a "stalemate of norms."[6]

At the same time, the international information security debate has long been characterized by mutual blind spots. Unless directly engaged with Russia, China, or the ITU, many in the United States and allied policy or academic communities remain simply unaware that there is a view that diverges sharply from the one they are accustomed to.

In part, this is because of the striking unanimity of view on the subject among English-speaking nations, where it is hard to identify any divergence in approach and underlying assumptions on the role and nature of cyber security. This deep consensus can give rise to a situation where even those experts with international exposure can overlook the fact that this is not the only possible view. For example, attendees at the launch of the *Tallinn Manual* referred to previously at the Royal Institute of International Affairs (Chatham House) in London, UK, in March 2013, heard the following description of its universal acceptance: "The U.S., the UK, the EU [European Union], and NATO [North Atlantic Treaty Organization] all agree. Everybody agrees"[7] — rather overlooking that "everybody" includes substantially more nations with a very different approach to the subject.

The broad divide between those states and organizations that argue that new international law is required to govern cyberspace and cyber conflict, and those that are satisfied with existing law, is a convenient tool for explaining the broad sweep of the debate, but it masks complexities. For example, the Russian and Chinese approaches to the problem can appear superficially similar — sufficiently so for Russia and China to cooperate on drafting the "International Code of Conduct" referred to previously. But within this alternative consensus, there are nuances and variations. As noted by Bertrand de La Chapelle, Director of the Internet & Jurisdiction Project at the International Diplomatic Academy in Paris and a Director on the Internet Corporation for Assigned Names and Numbers (ICANN) Board, although the debate on Internet governance:

> externally resembles an institutional battle . . . between institutions progressively put in place to ensure the growth of internet infrastructure, including ICANN, and the traditional multilateral system of the United Nations (UN) and its specialized agencies, including the International Telecommunications Union (ITU). . . . this vision is dangerous . . . and also erroneous and over-simplified. The approaches of the various actors are infinitely more complex.[8]

For this reason, the Russian approach to legality in cyberspace needs to be considered separately from that of China, the SCO, the Collective Security Treaty Organization, or any other state or organization whose views appear at first sight to chime with the Russian ones.

Why Cyber Security Is Needed.

In order to assess the Russian approach to what is and is not permissible in cyberspace, it is essential first to deal with a mismatch of fundamental notions of cyber security. Even before we approach the topic of actual cyber conflict, the official Russian view is that cyber security overall is not about defending businesses and people, as we would understand it, but states and territories. So to understand the Russian viewpoint, we need to leave behind some of the basic assumptions and principles about cyberspace stated by Euro-Atlantic governments.

For the purpose of illustration, we can avoid well-known U.S. statements on cyber security and instead take Sweden as a case study. According to Swedish Ministry of Foreign Affairs officials from the International Law and Human Rights Department:

> We analyze internet freedom within a human rights framework. . . . The foundation is basic human rights law: security needs to be arranged so as not to violate human rights law . . . Information security is to protect the individual, not governments. It's to protect you and me.[9]

This notion that human rights are a fundamental concern determining how the Internet should be managed contrasts with the Russian approach voiced in public statements that security is an essential basis and other considerations are secondary. In fact, as will be discussed herein, specific activities that Sweden encourages on the Internet are interpreted by Russia as hostile actions.

Sweden is not the only country that disagrees with the Russian approach that security trumps all other considerations when using the Internet. The UK view is that economic issues are the foundation, and security has to be built around these: "Cyber is first about the economy and prosperity. National security and military security are not the most immediate concerns there."[10]

The overall UK assumption that cyber security is "to protect the individual, not governments" overlaps with, but does not equate to, the standard Russian formulation of security being about protection of the trinity of individual, society, and state.[11] As will be seen in repeated examples throughout this Letort Paper, this balance of interests in the Russian perception leads to a highly distinctive Russian approach to what is permissible and legal in cyberspace.

THE EURO-ATLANTIC CONSENSUS

What follows is not a qualified legal opinion, but rather refers to a number of existing analyses to describe a general consensus. This will provide context and contrast for the description of the Russian approach that follows.

Cyber Warfare and International Law.

Many current legal debates in the United States and allied countries over conflict in cyberspace center on the definition of an "armed attack" or "use of force," and how these definitions can be extended into cyberspace. This is because Article 2(4) of the UN Charter prohibits the threat or use of force (undefined) against the territorial integrity or political independence of any state—except (Article 51) in cases of self-defense against an armed attack (also undefined). The lack of clarity over what constitutes an armed attack in cyberspace raises complications in other spheres as well, such as its use in the North Atlantic Treaty as a criterion for collective action by NATO.

Thus there is a basic gap in fundamental definitions for deciding what is, and is not, legal in cyber warfare. According to one detailed analysis of the existing law governing cyber conflict:

> Right now, no comprehensive international treaty exists to regulate cyber attacks. Consequently, states must practice law by analogy: either equating cyber attacks to traditional armed attacks and responding to them under the law of war or equating them to criminal activity and dealing with them under domestic criminal laws.[12]

But this is considered broadly satisfactory. Customary international law has come to take the view that armed attack requires a certain intensity, and a response in self-defense requires necessity and proportionality. Anticipatory self-defense is based on imminence, but the burden of proof lies with the actor that responds in self-defense. Thus the lack of absolute definition of hostile activity in cyberspace does not exonerate a state that has acted in a hostile manner:

> Every internationally wrongful act by a State gives rise to international responsibility. . . . Conduct consisting of an action or omission is imputed to a State under international law. . . . The basis of state responsibility will vary with the content of the international obligation. This may be a strict basis or the basis of risk in some circumstances, while in others it may involve malice or culpable negligence, or, conceivably, malice.[13]

So, it is argued:

> States have a right under international law to: 1. View and respond to cyber attacks as acts of war and not solely as criminal matters. 2. Use active, not just passive, defenses against the computer networks in other states, that may or may not have initiated an attack, but have neglected their duty to prevent cyber attacks from within their borders.[14]

This latter point addresses an issue long thought contentious in cyberspace, namely responsibility for the actions of nonstate actors. In fact, nonstate actors who carry out hostile actions against foreign states (particularly relevant in the case of Russia) are also provided for by existing legal obligations. According to one analysis:

> Since it is not realistic to expect states to completely prevent armed attacks by non-state actors, the dispositive factor in evaluating state conduct is what a state does to address potential threats and whether it takes realistic steps to prevent the attack from occurring.[15]

States have a longstanding duty to prevent non-state actors from using their territory to commit cross-border attacks. Traditionally, this duty only required states to prevent illegal acts that the state knew about beforehand. However, this duty has evolved in response to international terrorism and now requires states to act against groups generally known to carry out illegal acts. In the realm of cyber warfare, this duty should be interpreted to require states to enact and enforce criminal laws to deter cross-border cyber attacks. This means that:

> Either states will live up to their duty and start enforcing criminal laws against attackers, or states will violate their duty, which will create a legal pathway for victim-states to hold them legally responsible for an attack without having to attribute it first. In effect, repeated failure by a state to take criminal action against its attackers will result in it being declared a 'sanctuary state,' allowing other states to use active defenses against cyber attacks originating from within its borders.[16]

By extension, another highly contentious issue, that of positive attribution of hostile cyber activity to identify the perpetrator and take appropriate responsive action against the correct target, is also addressed partially addressed in the case of nonstate actors:

> It is evident that victim-states may forcibly respond to armed attacks by non-state actors located in another state when host-states violate their duty to prevent those attacks. With cyber attacks, imputing state responsibility in this manner provides states a legal path to utilize active defenses without having to conclusively attribute an attack to a state or its agents.[17]

In short, if a state "looks the other way when cyber attacks are conducted against rival states, it effectively breaches its duty to prevent them through its unwillingness to do anything to stop them, just as if it had approved the attacks."[18]

At the same time, in order for Law of Armed Conflict (LOAC) to apply to a particular conflict, neither formal declaration of war nor recognition of a state of war is required. According to a detailed analysis of the legal status of cyber activity during the armed conflict in Georgia in 2008, this was subject to the requirements of LOAC "as from the actual opening of hostilities."[19] An analysis of ethics applicable to cyber warfare agrees:

> Because the principle of forfeiture determines permissible responses to all interpersonal harm, the point at which kinetic and cyber-attacks constitute a just cause or *casus belli* is the same.[20]

and continues by describing further analogies that can determine a *casus belli*:

> On the one hand, a person attempting or actively intending to murder through a series of harms known to be individually non-lethal but lethal in aggregate is liable to lethal force. On the other hand, successive cyber-intrusions that combine to merely weaken a state militarily and/or economically do not in themselves constitute a just cause for war.[21]

As can be seen, the legal debate is complex and multifaceted. By contrast, one Russian argument is that efforts should be made not to regulate cyber warfare, but to outlaw it altogether.

RUSSIAN VIEWS

In contrast to the common Western view of the Internet as an enabler and facilitator, many Russian analysts, experts, and commentators are guided by a much better established perception of insecurity online, and a greater openness to considering the Internet as a vulnerability as well as an opportunity. The Russian intelligence services publicly stress the potential for a detrimental effect on national security arising from connection to the Internet.[22] According to Associate Professor of the Faculty of Electronic Warfare of the Russian Combined-Arms Academy Pavel Antonovich, not only does Russia risk seeing a:

> negative effect on how its national interests are safeguarded [resulting from] improvements in the form of unlawful activity in the cybernetic . . . area, and in high technologies" — but these technologies themselves are a threat.[23] Other authoritative writers in the prestigious "Military Thought" journal stress not only the asymmetric effect of cyber attack on Russia —

> The information infrastructures of major powers such as the U.S. or the Russian Federation could be wrecked hopelessly by a single battalion of 600 "cyber fighters" after two years of training for a cyber attack and no more than $100 million in costs.[24]

Antonovich concluded by summarizing the impact on society and the state as a whole, over and above our preoccupation with the direct effect on specific targets:

> The damage done by cyber weapons may include man-made disasters at vital industrial, economic, power, and transportation facilities, financial collapse,

and systemic economic crisis. Besides, cyber weapons can cause government and military operations to spin completely out of control, leave the population demoralized and disorientated, and set off widespread panic.[25]

The alarm voiced by the security services is not a new concern that has arrived with the rise of social media, but a persistent narrative since the first public debates on the subject in the mid-1990s, when the Internet as a whole was described by the Federal Security Service (FSB, Russian secret police) as a threat to Russian national security. A consistent argument since that time has been that Russian connection to the "world information space . . . is impossible without the comprehensive resolution of the problems of information security."[26] More recently, the perception of vulnerability to hostile activity using the medium of the Internet has become ever more acute: as argued in 2012, "this is not an empty scare—the cyberspace warfare is already on."[27]

This perception of vulnerability lends even greater weight to the habitual Russian emphasis on international law being the essential framework underpinning all international activity.[28] This accent on the primacy of law is typically much more prominent than in U.S. and allied statements, and although it does rest on a distinctive view of the nature of international law,[29] it also in part explains the Russian persistence in seeking new international legal instruments governing cyberspace.

The Russian argument for a new "Convention on International Information Security," which would also govern aspects of what we would describe as cyber warfare, has been exhaustively deconstructed elsewhere.[30] The remainder of this section will examine the underlying Russian ideas and preconceptions that illustrate points of divergence from U.S. and Euro-Atlantic approaches. This will be done in three distinct areas: domestic application of existing law; the military approach; and the results for how Russia's international legal initiatives are presented and received.

Domestic Application.

There is a widespread perception outside Russia that Internet use there is heavily censored, and that freedom of expression is suppressed as a result of a misguided and paranoid view among the Russian security services that free speech constitutes a threat to the ruling regime. As always, the real picture is more complex and nuanced.

An example of the distinctive nature of the Russian approach, and the security considerations behind it, comes with the use of social media. Emphasis on freedom of expression as a human right causes some foreign observers to suffer an allergic reaction when exposed to official Russian statements that appear to call for regulation of expression on social media. These statements, while they may appear entirely rational within context, are received overseas in an environment in which freedom of expression is sacrosanct, and which finds it inconceivable that social media, as a means of that expression, can be subject to restriction.

This conviction is so deep that some nations take upon themselves a mission to assist this free expression in other countries, regardless of whether this is in accordance with those countries' national law. Returning to the case of Sweden, 20 percent of the Swedish overseas development budget is spent on "capacity building/democracy support" — including "providing tools needed to communicate successfully" in repressive environments and "providing encryption software for activists" to ensure this communication remains concealed from the national government and law enforcement authorities.[31]

This is precisely the kind of interference in another state's "information space" that Russia views as hostile and wishes to proscribe through international agreements like the "Convention" referenced previously. At a UN disarmament conference in 2008, a Russian Ministry of Defence representative suggested that any time a government promoted ideas on the Internet with the intention of subverting another country's government, including in the name of democratic reform, this would qualify as "aggression" and an interference in internal affairs.[32] Yet at the same time, this is not construed by Sweden as a hostile act. According to Carl Fredrik Wettermark of the International Law and Human Rights Department, Swedish Ministry of Foreign Affairs (MFA), "there is no tension between democracy support — including encryption and communications provision — and working with the governments that the activists are opposing."[33]

This fundamental contradiction arises in part because of an almost total lack of threat perception arising from social media among the Euro-Atlantic community. Fortunately, a case study is available to demonstrate why Russia and other nations are concerned over misuse of social media — or why, as expressed by Major General Aleksey Moshkov of the Russian Ministry of Internal Affairs in late 2011, "social networks, along with advantages, often bring a potential threat to the foundations of society."[34] This is the case of the uprising and civil war in Libya, where social media and online communication circumventing government control played a key role in regime change. According to a study published by the U.S. Naval War College:

> Successful dispute of the government control of communications led to freedom of action in the cyber and land domains. This freedom of action led to traditional military support from the U.S. and NATO that ultimately allowed the opposition to achieve the physical objectives of defeating the Gaddafi regime and the eventual election of a new government.[35]

Translated to the context of Russian security concerns, this correlates to statements like the one by FSB First Deputy Director Sergei Smirnov in early 2012: "New technologies are used by Western secret services to create and maintain a level of continual tension in society with serious intentions extending even to regime change."[36]

The view that political change in North Africa after the Arab Spring came about as a result of a Western IW and cyber conspiracy, which could then be implemented against Russia, fed into suspicion of foreign orchestration at the time of Russia's election protests in 2011-12, and was subsequently vindicated by analyses (like the one mentioned previously) of the role of social media in the Libyan civil war—which showed that they can be used not only for the espionage, subversion, and circumvention of communications restrictions suspected by Russia's security services,[37] but also for other instruments of regime change, up to and including supplying targeting information for airstrikes.[38] Assessment of Russian concerns over "misuse" of social media needs to be placed in the context of this perception of existential threat.

A complicating factor that hinders understanding of the official Russian attitude to the legality of domestic Internet use is that policy statements on this and other issues differ widely depending on their source, giving rise to yet more incomprehension abroad. Officials from bodies including the MFA, the Ministry of Internal Affairs, the Ministry of Communications, the FSB, the Security Council, and the Presidential Administration (the latter two, voiced through their academic offshoots, the Institute of Information Security Issues and the Russian Institute for Strategic Studies, respectively) make pronouncements that rightly or wrongly are seen as voicing official Russian government policy, and which are mutually contradictory. For this reason and others, commercial entities in Russia and those following the topic overseas eagerly await the promised release of a new cyber security strategy, which should clarify at least some of the more controversial issues.

When Russian proposals are reviewed overseas, a further perceived incompatibility arises between Russian initiatives for international action on cyber security and Russia's own bad reputation as a permissive environment for cyber crime. A book published in 2011 stated that:

> Given the strength of . . . comprehensive surveillance of the Internet, one might assume that Russia would represent an implacably hostile environment for cyber criminals. Yet the Russian Federation has become one of the great centers of global cybercrime. The strike rate of the police is lamentable, while the number of those convicted barely reaches double figures.
>
> The reason, while unspoken, is largely understood. Russian cyber criminals are free . . . provided the tar-

get of [their] attacks are located in Western Europe and the United States.[39]

This statement appeared entirely uncontroversial because of a relative lack of publicity for recent Russian efforts against cyber crime and the high profile of commercial entities, as opposed to law-enforcement agencies, in combating crime. The impression abroad persists, therefore, that there has been no change in the (at the very least) permissive attitude to cyber crime and to other forms of antisocial behavior online, including the activities of "patriotic hackers" carrying out destructive and criminal activity in foreign states such as Estonia and Georgia, activity that happens to coincide with the Russian state aims of the day. Indeed, Russia's perceived unwillingness to prosecute cyber crime against overseas targets has been put forward as a serious and plausible explanation for the concurrent unwillingness to join the Budapest Convention on Cybercrime.[40]

The department of Russia's Ministry of Internal Affairs that deals with cyber crime is referred to as "Directorate K." Russia was slow to legislate against computer crime, and this department is, to some extent, still hampered by inadequate and outdated legislation. Colonel General (Retired) Boris Nikolayevich Miroshnikov, the cultured and softly spoken first commander of Directorate K, explains that "our laws are not keeping up with the problems we are observing. . . . [W]e are the victims of our civil legal regulation not keeping up.[41]

In part, he says, this results from pursuing the economic benefits of the Internet while disregarding security concerns — echoing criticism by other Russian commentators of the Western approach to use of the

Internet. In addition, the pace of developing new laws is simply unable to keep up with the development of activity in cyberspace. "An event has to become a phenomenon, then we have to study it, then legislate — but we are in a legal lacuna between the old and new laws," Miroshnikov says.[42] The result is palpable frustration at the balance of legislation governing online activity, with officials citing the example of banks that have been victims of cyber crime responding to requests for information with the aim of assisting them, with a detailed legal explanation of why this information cannot be given due to legislation on commercial secrecy and protection of personal data. The situation is complicated still further by competition between Russian law enforcement agencies, investigators, and prosecutors, a situation referred to by Boris Miroshnikov as "departmental egoism."[43]

New laws governing Internet usage have recently been passed in Russia. These laws tend to attract criticism from abroad. Both a July 2013 law on protection of intellectual property online, and the July 2012 "Internet blacklist" law setting up a "Single Register" of websites blocked because they are deemed threatening to minors, have been painted by activists and foreign media as state efforts to introduce Internet censorship on ostensibly economic and moral grounds — including, potentially, censorship of social media outlets.[44] But it is misleading to present these laws solely as an initiative intended to stifle political dissent. They also variously meet international and domestic commercial obligations, and reflect a desire to preserve some elements of Russian cultural norms. Many more proposals for doing so have been raised in the Russian legislative bodies but fallen flat on the grounds of impracticality, such as a draft law that would have outlawed foul language on the Internet.[45] The suggestion that legislation has been introduced at the request of President Putin to suppress dissent is undermined by the continuing proliferation of sometimes quite mordant anti-Putin satire online.[46]

Detailed assessments of the impact, intended and unintended, of legislative initiatives is provided by the Russian Association for Electronic Communications (RAEC), an industrial body that provides expert evaluations for draft laws and provides a voice for the Internet industry in shaping the regulatory picture.[47] These assessments can differ markedly from the sometimes overblown rhetoric of rights organizations and overseas media when discussing the same legislation.

In addition, fears of sweeping powers to remove offending content from the Internet, if not misplaced, are perhaps mistimed: these powers were already available to the Russian authorities through legal and regulatory routes. Under the Federal law "On Police" dated 2011, Internet service providers can be instructed to shut down an Internet resource on suspicion of providing "conditions which assist the commission of a crime or administrative violation," with no requirement for the police to seek a court order. According to Russian domain name regulations, "the Registrar may terminate the domain name delegation on the basis of a decision in writing" by a senior law enforcement official—again, with no requirement for judicial oversight.[48]

Despite allegations that the Single Register has been used to censor or stifle views critical of the government, the loudest criticism comes from those who note that it is a blunt instrument whose flawed implementation has serious unintended consequences—for instance, blocking YouTube because a zombie make-up instruction video is wrongly identified as promoting self-harm, or rendering Russia's most popular search engine, Yandex, unavailable for almost 30 minutes in late April 2013 due to its being accidentally added to the Register.[49]

These criticisms are often directed at the Ministry of Communications, as the body with ultimate supervisory authority for the Register. The Ministry response, far from the hard line that critics of Russia often assume, is that it is asking the Internet industry to self-regulate, and the Single Register is a mechanism for this — and furthermore, the Ministry should not be blamed, as it is only implementing a Federal law rather than its own regulations.

It follows that the nature of control of freedom of expression online in Russia is more subtle and nuanced than the heavy-handed censorship often described overseas, and it would be misleading to claim that the sole aim of recent legal initiatives is to suppress dissent.[50] At the same time, the fundamentally different Russian approach to the balance of rights and responsibilities online remains. The head of the Russian MFA's Department of New Challenges and Threats (which, naturally, includes cyber) — and Russia's cyber ambassador — is Andrey Vladimirovich Krutskikh. In his view, the primacy of freedom of speech that is promoted by Western powers is a form of "extremism," and its damaging potential is incompatible with freedom of access to the Internet.[51] Krutskikh uses the example of Boston police requesting social media users not to broadcast police activities in the aftermath of the Boston marathon bombing in April 2013[52] to bolster his argument for the need to regulate freedom of expression in the interests of national security.[53] Thus the distinctive official Russian view of cyber security continues to be informed by a perception of threat from the Internet, and of the balance of interest there, which is at odds with our own.

Military Views.

According to the former head of the Russian General Staff's Main Operations Directorate, Lieutenant General Andrey Tretyak, there are now four "spaces for high-technology confrontation—space, land, air, and information."[54] When considering Russian approaches to cyber, it is essential to remember the different dividing lines between information operations and computer network operations that pertain to Russian thinking, and the resulting references to "information space" rather than cyberspace.[55]

Russian writing in open sources on the likely nature of online confrontation—including, for example, the *Conceptual Views on the Activity of the Russian Federation Armed Forces in Information Space*, a document widely seen as the Russian military's cyber proto-doctrine—rarely fail to refer to the need to observe legalities. For example, a 2012 essay on military thought regarding rules and principles governing this kind of conflict:

> If, however, a conflict heats up to a critical point, the Russian Armed Forces will exercise their right to individual or collective self-defense and resort to any methods and weapons they choose, as long as they comply with the commonly accepted norms and principles of international law.[56]

Yet over and above the issue of a specific Russian interpretation of existing international law, there is also the consideration of at what point Russia considers itself to be at war and therefore subject to *jus in bello*. Recent Russian commentary stresses the blurring of the distinction between war and peace, and asks to what extent this distinction still exists. Antonovich, cited previously, argues that cyberspace erodes this line and holds that actions in cyberspace are allowed without crossing the line to war. Significantly, he argues that damaging cyber attacks can be carried out without a state of war existing or being triggered by the attack:

> Dividing lines between war and peace can be eroded conveniently in cyberspace. Damage (whatever its nature) can actually be done to an adversary without overstepping formally the line between war and peace.[57]

This suggestion of a shifting boundary between war and peace is not restricted to academic circles: the same idea was voiced by Chief of General Staff Valeriy Gerasimov when he contended at a speech for the Academy of Military Sciences that the states of war and peace are now more of a continuum than distinct, and that new types of conflict other than war can have political results comparable to war.[58]

Gerasimov's argument is worth studying in detail, not only for its possible implications for cyber conflict, but also for understanding Russia's approach to the use of armed force overall. The new continuum of conflict is explained in detail by Vladimir Makhonin, a Russian historian who describes a hierarchy of conflict where war is the ultimate stage but is preceded by armed conflict, which in its turn is preceded by social conflict (defined as resolving, by a variety of means, extreme differences). In other words, social conflict and armed attack take their place as a stage of confrontation that do not, according to this view, amount to war.[59]

The implications of this for cyber conflict are two-fold. First, any full-scale cyber conflict would, just as with conventional armed conflict, be preceded by smaller-scale attacks:

> It may be safely assumed that a large-scale external aggression aimed at seizing Russia's resources will be preceded by a series of conflicts (*not necessarily armed ones*) within the country. Increasing activity by various terrorist, ethnic separatist, extremist and other similar organizations will become a species of reconnaissance in force as the situation ripens for a large-scale war. Historical experience suggests that this kind of scenario is only too feasible.[60]

Second, hostile information activity, including computer network operations, can be conducted outside a state of war. According to an exceptional study of Russian views on information operations and IW by Sweden's Defence Research Agency (FOI):

> Regarding network and computer operations in peacetime IW, viruses and other malware are important in order to compromise the information assets of the engineering systems of the enemy. Other aspects of IW are accumulating (stealing) information on the enemy, by intelligence gathering, while developing and testing one's own IW weapons.[61]

This is a departure from previous Russian views of the status of information warfare. In the mid-1990s, leading experts Timothy L. Thomas and Lester Grau were able to write that:

> . . . from a military point, the view of Information Warfare against Russia or its armed forces will categorically not be considered a non-military phase of a conflict whether it will be causalities or not . . . considering the possible catastrophic use of information warfare means by an enemy, whether on economic or state command and control systems, or on the combat potential of the armed forces. . . . Russia retains the right to use nuclear weapons first against the means and forces of information warfare, and then against the aggressor state itself.[62]

Three further specific features of current Russian views on when cyber force can legitimately be used need to be briefly considered. First, there is the nature of the threat perceived by Russia, its radical difference from Western threat perception, and its pervasive influence on decisionmaking. As noted by Stephen Blank and others, "We often underestimate the impact of the Russian leadership's perception that Russia is intrinsically at risk, and in some sense under attack from the West."[63] Second, and related to the first, there is Russian awareness of a capability gap with the threatening West, and the consequent need to respond asymmetrically. Norwegian analyst Tor Bukkvoll writes that:

> The idea of developing an asymmetric technological response—popular in many nations with more or less strained relations with the West—has become a truism among the Russian traditionalists. The main reason is the realization that the Western lead is too great to catch up with.[64]

Indeed, according to Vladimir Putin, Russia's responses to threats "are to be based on intellectual superiority. They will be asymmetrical, and less costly."[65] Third, there is the distinctive Russian perception of its relations with its smaller neighbors—including those that are commonly held to have been targets of Russian cyber attacks, Estonia and Georgia. A separate Norwegian study of Russian attitudes to the use of force was published in 2005, before any widely publicized cyber aggression was ascribed to Russia. But its conclusion regarding conventional intervention is just as valid for cyber: "It can be argued that Russian decisionmakers simply did not consider the former Soviet republics foreign in terms of cases of intervention."[66]

International Initiatives.

Russia has persistently sought a new international legal instrument that would constrain activity in cyberspace. The desire for this is driven by considerations described previously, including threat perception, emphasis on the primacy of international law, and a Russian desire to constrain competitors by political means while in a state of vulnerability arising from a capability gap.[67] There is also the traditional debate over the relative weight of the capabilities or the intentions of potential adversaries. For Andrey Krutskikh, the answer is clear: "Imagine that 120-130 countries acquire the capability for cyber strikes— then the strikes will inevitably follow."[68] This section will not list specific points of the Russian proposals, as this has been done in detail elsewhere:[69] instead, it looks at how they are presented and received, and the implications of this for the United States and its allies.

There is an apparent paradox that some widely accepted international agreements are already available, but not subscribed to by Russia. This is because, as drafted, they contain clauses that are unacceptable to the Russian authorities. As noted by OSCE experts Raphael Perl and Nemanja Malisevic, some states do have legitimate objections to clauses in instruments such as the Council of Europe's Convention on Cybercrime 2001 (the Budapest Convention): "in reality . . . many states face challenges in becoming party to these conventions."[70]

Initiatives put forward by Russia for international cooperation in information security have received a mixed response from other states. In particular, over a period of years they have been consistently ignored or rejected by the United States, the UK, and other like-minded nations. This response is indicative of the huge remaining divide between the views and assumptions expressed in these Russian initiatives and the Euro-Atlantic presumptions, which are taken for granted by many of those reading them.[71]

Experts involved in discussions with Russia, or analysis of their proposals, are able to engage in debate over their specific provisions, their acceptability to the United States and allies, and their practicality or otherwise. But remember that this international group with exposure to both sides of the argument is only a very small subset of the much larger group of individuals engaged with the issues as a whole. Many more officials, diplomats, policymakers, and advisers in Western nations will only be acquainted with their own side of the debate. The reaction to Russian statements, actions, and policy initiatives from this group can include words like: unpredictable, unnecessarily uncooperative, incomprehensible, and frequently, irrational.

In part, this is because of the relative lack of visibility abroad of key Russian proposals. Opportunities to bring the Russian ideas to broader notice appear often not to be taken. We can take as an example the Budapest Conference on Cyberspace in October 2012, on the face of it a prime venue for explaining the Russian point of view to the world. Ahead of the conference, "International Cyber Documents" were provided for reference on its website, outlining national and international approaches to cyber security—for example, the text of a speech by Swedish Foreign Minister Carl Billet, Australian and Canadian white papers and cyber security strategies, the Budapest Convention on Cybercrime, OECD recommendations, and NATO statements. Yet no Russian equivalent was provided.[72] During the conference itself, just as at the London Conference on Cyberspace the previous year, a presentation delivered in Russian failed to account for interpretation and therefore failed to put across key points at which the Russian view diverged from the Euro-Atlantic consensus on the nature of the Internet and rights and obligations in cyberspace. It was for this reason, among others, that many observers experienced considerable surprise when this consensus came face to face with the rest of the world at the World Conference on International Telecommunications (WCIT) in Dubai in December 2012.

A key lesson from WCIT for those who had not been following the debate was the extent of support for the viewpoint championed by Russia from those countries that share similar concerns about the cyber threat. Although Russian initiatives have been mostly discounted or ignored in the West, this is not their only audience, and Russia has been busy gathering support from other countries not usually considered cyber powers, but with a perfectly valid vote in fora such as the ITU or the UN. This is possible because while many of the proposals appear counterintuitive, outdated, unworkable, or otherwise unacceptable to a Western audience, they appear comforting and reasonable in parts of the world that see a potential threat in the unrestricted circulation of information, including hostile and damaging information, both domestically and internationally.

At the same time, while many of the proposals for international agreement, and the assumptions about the nature of the Internet that underlie them, are in direct conflict with how the Euro-Atlantic community understands the Internet to work, they also conflict with the understanding of Russian Internet authorities themselves at a working level. For instance, a key principle of the Russian proposals is the concept of national information space under state control. But this is not compatible with the work of Russian Internet service providers and domain authorities, unrelated to the state, who ensure the free circulation of information across borders on a daily basis, because this is a fundamental feature of the Internet. As stated on the website of the Russian Internet Governance Forum (RIGF), which took place in late April 2013:

Интернет является надгосударственным образованием и, де- факто, не имеет границ. Именно поэтому для интернета так подходит модель коллективного управления Сетью (т.н. мультистейк-холдеризм)

(The internet is a supra-governmental entity, and de facto has no borders. It is for this reason that the model of collective governance [so-called multistakeholderism] is so suitable for the internet.)[73]

This is in direct contradiction to some key principles of Russian initiatives at a political level.

The points mentioned thus far create an unforgiving environment for positive reception of Russia's ideas on the nature and purpose of cyber security, and they contribute to the lack of meaningful debate on what precisely those ideas are. This leads to their rejection, either instinctive or reasoned, by Western liberal readers. Russia's proposed Draft Convention on International Information Security, as well as the International Code of Conduct proposed by Russia and other states in the UN, are the latest iteration of longstanding proposals but remain unacceptable to the Euro-Atlantic community.

In fact, as explained by a Nordic diplomat speaking anonymously, some states deliberately avoid any use of the term "information security" in official statements because of its negative associations; even if the phrase is the most appropriate one to describe the topic under discussion, it has been sufficiently tainted by association with the regulatory stance adopted by Russia and China in particular, that it is shunned in favor of the more acceptable "cyber security." Meanwhile, official representatives of other states that are deeply cautious about naming specific states as cyber security offenders overall can casually refer to Russia and China as the "worst adversaries" — not in cyber conflict, but in discussion over human rights.[74]

At a public level, examples abound of a total failure to achieve not just dialogue, but also the level of mutual comprehension that would be its essential precursor. The dialogue of the deaf continues, with a failure on each side to appreciate how the other will perceive statements. This includes a lack of understanding that policy taken as normal and uncontroversial in the West can appear threatening in Russia and in other parts of the world as well. For instance, when Giuseppe Abbamonte of the European Commission's Directorate General for Communications Networks, Content and Technology states publicly that a key part of the EU cyber security strategy is "engaging with third parties and **making sure that we export our values**," many of those hearing him will not take into account that substantial parts of the world do not wish to have their values exported from Brussels[75] — and, in fact, precisely this kind of export is construed as a direct information security threat in Russia's Information Security Doctrine.[76]

The opposite also applies. Those following Russian statements in the same field have to contend not only with the multiple and conflicting sources of apparent policy initiatives as described previously, but also with accompanying statements, which can leave them disinclined to take what they read seriously — as, for instance, with the following response to moves for improved protection of intellectual property online:

> Is the world about to allow the US and its surrogates to come after all of us? Apparently it is. The total enslavement of mankind will soon be here, brought to you by the fascist United Corporate States of America.[77]

It is true that commentary in the media should not necessarily be taken as representative of an official Russian position, but this point is harder to argue when the name of the media outlet is "Voice of Russia."

The result of this disconnect between radically different approaches to the same issue can be compared to other areas of strategic contention between Russia and the Euro-Atlantic community, such as Russia's proposals for a new European Security Treaty or Russian objections to plans for basing missile defense systems in and around Europe. In all of these cases, the Russian position is based on considerations and assumptions that are wholly incompatible with reality as the European and North American audience understands it. The result, in many cases, is that what often seems the simplest and most appropriate response to them is not to engage with the incomprehensible Russian view, but simply to ignore it and hope it will go away. Unfortunately, as can be seen from the other two longstanding examples given here, this tends not to happen.

CONCLUSION

The distinctive Russian approach to what is permissible, and indeed moral, in cyberspace has implications for U.S. policymakers in two key areas. First, there is consideration of the response to Russian and similar proposals for international agreements governing cyberspace. As noted, in common with other longstanding Russian diplomatic initiatives, these proposals will remain in place regardless of whether their audience sees them as unworkable or indeed incomprehensible. But unlike in previous years, it is no longer safe to broadly ignore them, due to the growing alternative consensus on cyber security that opposes the view of the United States and its close allies. Thus, if the United States wishes to see its own concept of Internet freedom to remain the dominant one, the diplomatic momentum that allowed a "formidable" U.S. delegation to attend WCIT needs to be maintained, and engagement needs to be fostered on a multilateral basis to counter the effective Russian program of ticking up support for Moscow's proposals from other countries around the world.

Second, there is the specific question of when, or whether, hostile action in cyberspace constitutes an act or state of war. On this point, Russian thinking appears at odds with the emerging Western consensus. This requires an expansion of study of law both within the U.S. military and in academia to include active consideration of the view from Russia and other dissenting nations. Achieving direct dialogue between the U.S. and Russian militaries, as well as with other agencies on the Russian side that would be engaged in cyber conflict, may be challenging but must be attempted. Confidence building measures to avert cyber conflict can expand on agreements reached between the United States and Russia during June 2013 that were "dedicated to assessing emerging ICT [information and communication technologies] threats and proposing concrete joint measures to address them,"[78] including provision for direct communications between national community emergency response teams (CERTs).[79]

Finally, U.S. policymakers cannot afford to underestimate the extent to which Russian concepts and approaches differ from what they may take for granted. For instance, much effort has been devoted in the West to determining when a cyber weapon can legally be used.[80] But when engaging in debate with Russia, we must consider that even the notion of what constitutes a cyber weapon—or in Russian terminology, an information weapon—will be radically different from our assumptions.[81] As put over a decade ago by the eminent scholar of Russian ways of thinking Timothy L. Thomas:

What is really different is the conceptual understanding of an information operation from a cultural, ideological, historical, scientific, and philosophical viewpoint. Different prisms of logic may offer totally different conclusions about an information operation's intent, purpose, lethality, or encroachment on sovereignty; and this logic may result in new methods to attack targets in entirely non-traditional and creative ways.[82]

ENDNOTES

1. *The Tallinn Manual on the International Law Applicable to Cyber Warfare*, Cambridge, UK: Cambridge University Press, 2013, available from *www.ccdcoe.org/249.html*.

2. Jason Healey, ed., *A Fierce Domain: Conflict in Cyberspace, 1986 to 2012*, Washington, DC: Cyber Conflict Studies Association and Atlantic Council, 2013.

3. Jaroslav Sirjajev, "Cyberterrorism in the Context of Contemporary International Law," *San Diego International Law Journal*, Vol. 14, No. 139, 2012; Raphael Perl and Nemanja Malisevic, "A Comprehensive Approach to Cyber Security — Trends, Challenges and the Way Forward," in John J. Le Beau, ed., *The Dangerous Landscape: International Perspectives on Twenty-First Century Terrorism*, Garmisch-Partenkirchen, Germany: Partnership for Peace Consortium, 2013.

4. Perl and Malisevic.

5. Tom Miles, "Snowden affair is chance for truce in cyber war: U.N.," *Reuters*, July 15, 2013, available from *www.reuters.com/article/2013/07/15/net-us-usa-security-cybertruce-id USBRE96E0L320130715*.

6. Speaking at the Seventh Scientific Conference of the International Information Security Research Consortium, Garmisch-Partenkirchen, Germany, April 22-25, 2013.

7. Professor Michael N. Schmitt, general editor of *The Tallinn Manual on the International Law Applicable to Cyber Warfare,* speaking at the Royal Institute of International Affairs, Chatham House, London, UK, March 15, 2013.

8. Bertrand de La Chapelle, "Gouvernance Internet: tensions actuelles et futurs possibles" ("Internet governance: current tensions and possible futures"), in *Politique étrangère,* Vol. 2, No. 2012, Summer 2012, pp. 249-250.

9. Johan Hallenberg, Deputy Director, International Law and Human Rights Department, Swedish MFA, speaking at European Council on Foreign Relations, London, UK, April 17, 2013.

10. Kevin Tebbitt, former Director of Government Communications Headquarters (GCHQ) and Permanent Under Secretary of State for the UK Ministry of Defence, speaking at Global Strategy Forum, House of Lords, London, UK, November 21, 2012.

11. It should be noted that Russia is not the only nation to place less emphasis on the human rights aspect of cyber security. Insistence by European nations on highlighting rights at the Budapest Conference led to a Chinese question of whether the delegation was at a conference on cyber security or on human rights.

12. Matthew J. Sklerov, "Responding to international cyber attacks," in Jeffrey Carr, ed., *Inside Cyber Warfare: Mapping the Cyber Underworld,* Sebastopol, CA: O'Reilly, 2010, pp. 46-62.

13. Rosalyn Higgins, "Problems and Process: International Law and How We Use It," Oxford, UK: Oxford University Press, 1994, p. 149.

14. Matthew J. Sklerov, "Responding to international cyber attacks," in Jeffrey Carr, ed., *Inside Cyber Warfare: Mapping the Cyber Underworld,* Sebastopol, CA: O'Reilly, 2010, pp. 46-62.

15. *Ibid.*

16. *Ibid.*

17. *Ibid.*

18. *Ibid.*

19. Eneken Tikk, Kadri Kaska, Kristel Rünnimeri, Mari Kert, Anna-Maria Talihärm, and Liis Vihul, *Cyber Attacks Against Georgia: Legal Lessons Identified*, Tallinn, Estonia: NATO Cooperative Cyber Defence Centre of Excellence (CCDCOE), November 2008, p.19.

20. Edward T. Barrett, "Warfare in the new domain: the Ethics of Military Cyber-Operations," *Journal of Military Ethics*, Vol.12, No.1, 2013, pp. 4-17.

21. *Ibid.*

22. For more detail on this, see Keir Giles, "'Information Troops—A Russian Cyber Command?" Tallinn, Estonia: CCDCOE, June 2011.

23. Pavel Antonovich, "Cyberwarfare: Nature and Content," *Military Thought*, Vol. 20, No. 3, 2011, pp. 35-43.

24. S.I. Bazylev, I.N. Dylevsky, S.A. Komov, and A.N. Petrunin, "The Russian Armed Forces in the Information Environment: Principles, Rules, and Confidence-Building Measures," *Military Thought*, Vol. 21, No. 2, 2012, pp. 10-16.

25. *Ibid.*

26. Georgiy Smolyan, Vitaliy Tsygichko, and Dmitriy Chereshkin, "A Weapon That May Be More Dangerous Than a Nuclear Weapon: The Realities of Information Warfare," *Nezavisimoye voyennoye obozreniye*, November 18, 1995, pp. 1-2.

27. Bazylev *et al.*

28. Keir Giles, "Russia's Public Stance on Cyberspace Issues," C. Czosseck, R. Ottis, and K. Ziolkowski, eds., *2012 4th International Conference on Cyber Conflict*, Tallinn, Estonia, 2012.

29. Lauri Mälksoo, "International Law in Foreign Policy Documents of the Russian Federation: a Deconstruction," *Diplomaatia*, May 2011.

30. As, for instance, in "Russia's 'Draft Convention on International Information Security' — A Commentary," Oxford, UK: Conflict Studies Research Centre, April 2012, available from *conflictstudies.org.uk/files/20120426_CSRC_IISI_Commentary.pdf*.

31. Presentation by Swedish Ministry of Foreign Affairs officials, European Council on Foreign Relations (ECFR), London, UK, May 2013.

32. Giles, "Russia's Public Stance on Cyberspace Issues," p. 72.

33. Speaking in London, UK, May 2013.

34. Interviewed in *Rossiskaya Gazeta*, December 8, 2011.

35. John Scott-Railton, "Revolutionary Risks: Cyber Technology and Threats in the 2011 Libyan Rebellion," Newport, RI: U.S. Naval War College Center on Irregular Warfare and Armed Groups, 2013.

36. Speaking at a meeting of the Shanghai Cooperation Organization (SCO) Regional Anti-Terrorist Structure, March 27, 2012.

37. Daniel B. Prieto, "Are American spies the next victims of the Internet age?" *Foreign Policy*, August 9, 2013, available from *www.foreignpolicy.com/articles/2013/08/09/the_classifieds_open_source_intelligence_prieto?page=0,1*.

38. As with the reference to NATO's Intelligence Fusion Centre (NIFC) making use of Twitter:

> We get information from open sources on the Internet; we get Twitter. . . . You name any source of media and our fusion center will deliver all of that into usable intelligence.

Adam Gabbatt, "NATO, Twitter and air strikes in Libya," *Inside the Guardian* (blog), June 15, 2011, available from *www.guardian.co.uk/help/insideguardian/2011/jun/15/nato-twitter-libya*.

39. Misha Glenny, "DarkMarket: Cyberthieves, Cybercops and You," New York: Knopf, 2011.

40. Private author interviews, 2012-13.

41. Speaking at Seventh Scientific Conference of the International Information Security Research Consortium, Garmisch-Partenkirchen, Germany, April 22-25, 2013.

42. *Ibid.*

43. *Ibid.*

44. Katia Moskvitch, "Russia's anti-internet piracy law faces backlash," BBC, July 31, 2013 available from *www.bbc.com/news/technology-23510065.*

45. "Russia to ban foul language on social networks and discussion boards," *Pravda.ru*, July 26, 2013,available from *english.pravda.ru/society/family/26-07-2013/125277-foul_language-0/.*

46. For just one example among thousands, see the comedy group *Uralskiye Pelmeni*'s take on the presidential succession, available from *www.youtube.com/watch?feature=player_embedded&v=q48dB6NjHdY#t=13.*

47. *"Pravo v otrasli"* (Industry Law), RAEC, available from *raec.ru/right/.*

48. Presentation by Russian domain name registrar representative Alina Legoydo, Cyber Defence and Network Security conference, London, UK, January 26, 2012.

49. As was forcefully described by a Yandex official at the Russian Internet Governance Forum, Moscow, Russia, April 2013.

50. Keir Giles and Maxine David, "Cyber Security and Internet Protest," *Russian Analytical Digest*, Issue 134, July 30, 2013.

51. Seventh Scientific Conference of the International Information Security Research Consortium, Garmisch-Partenkirchen, Munich, Germany, April 22-25, 2013.

52. Timothy Stenovec, "Boston Police Scanner Live-Tweeting Complicates Manhunt For Second Suspected Marathon Bomber," *Huffington Post*, April 19, 2013, available from *www.huffingtonpost.com/2013/04/19/boston-police-scanner-live-tweeting-manhunt_n_3118253.html*.

53. Seventh Scientific Conference of the International Information Security Research Consortium.

54. Speaking in a briefing at NATO Defense College, Rome, Italy, November 27, 2012.

55. Keir Giles, "Divided by a Common Language: Cyber Definitions in Chinese, Russian and English," NATO CCDCOE, June 2013, available at *conflictstudies.org.uk/files/Cyber_Common_Language.pdf*.

56. Bazylev *et al.*, pp. 10-16.

57. Pavel Antonovich, "Cyberwarfare: Nature and Content," *Military Thought*, Vol. 20, No. 3, 2011, pp. 35-43.

58. Valeriy Gerasimov, "*Tsennost nauki v predvidenii*" ("The Value Of Science Is In Foresight"), *Voyenno-promyshlennyy kuryer*, No. 8, February 27, 2013, p. 476.

59. V. A. Makhonin, "How the Concepts of Military Conflict and War Are Related," *Military Thought*, Vol. 20, No. 4, 2010, pp. 152-155.

60. Shamil Aliyev, "Russia's Military Security and Social Conflicts," *Military Thought*, Vol. 19, No. 2, 2010, pp. 1-6.

61. Roland Heickerö, "Emerging Cyber Threats and Russian Views on Information Warfare and Information Operations," Swedish Defence Research Agency (FOI), 2010, p. 20, available from *www.foi.se/ReportFiles/foir_2970.pdf*.

62. Lester Grau, and Timothy L. Thomas, "A Russian View of Future War: Theory and Direction," *Journal of Slavic Military Studies*, Issue 9.3, September 1996, pp. 501–518.

63. Stephen J. Blank and Richard Weitz, eds., *The Russian Military Today and Tomorrow: Essays in Memory of Mary Fitzgerald,"* Carlisle, PA: Strategic Studies Institute, U.S. Army War College, 2010, p. 3.

64. Tor Bukkvoll, "Iron Cannot Fight—The Role of Technology in Current Russian Military Theory," *Journal of Strategic Studies*, Vol. 34, No. 5, 2011, pp. 681-706.

65. Vladimir Putin, *"Poslaniye Federal'nomu Sobraniyu Rossiyskoy Federatsii"* ("Address to the Federal Assembly of the Russian Federation"), as transcribed in *Krasnaya Zvezda*, No. 89, May 11, 2006.

66. Morten Langsholdt, "Russia and the Use of Force: Theory and Practice," Oslo, Norway: Norwegian Defence Research Establishment, Report 2005/02504, November 2005, available from *www.ffi.no/no/Rapporter/05-02504.pdf.*

67. Giles, "Information Troops."

68. Seventh Scientific Conference of the International Information Security Research Consortium.

69. "Russia's 'Draft Convention on International Information Security'—A Commentary," Sandhurst, UK: Conflict Studies Research Centre, April 2012, available from *conflictstudies.org.uk/files/20120426_CSRC_IISI_Commentary.pdf.*

70. Perl and Malisevic.

71. "Who Governs the Internet?" undated discussion paper, Global Partners & Associates, available at *www.gp-digital.org/wp-content/uploads/pubs/who-governs-internet_web2.pdf.*

72. See *www.cyberbudapest2012.hu/national-cyber-documents.*

73. Author's translation into English. See RIGF website available from *rigf.ru/about.*

74. Private conversations with author, April 2013.

75. Speaking at Cyber Defence and Network Security conference, London, UK, January 26, 2013, emphasis added.

76. According to the Information Security Doctrine of the Russian Federation, 2000, "spiritual, moral, and cultural values of citizens" should be protected from outside influence.

77. "Remember that MP3? The police are en-route," Voice of Russia website, December 10, 2012.

78. "U.S.-Russian Cooperation on Information and Communications Technology Security," Washington, DC: The White House, Office of the Press Secretary, June 17, 2013, available from *www.whitehouse.gov/the-press-office/2013/06/17/fact-sheet-us-russian-cooperation-information-and-communications-technol*.

79. Sean Gallagher, "US, Russia to install "cyber-hotline" to prevent accidental cyberwar," *Ars Technica*, June 18, 2013, available from *arstechnica.com/information-technology/2013/06/us-russia-to-install-cyber-hotline-to-prevent-accidental-cyberwar/*.

80. Stefano Mele, "Cyber-weapons: Legal and strategic aspects," *Defence IQ*, August 2013, available from *www.defenceiq.com/cyber-defence/white-papers/cyber-weapons-legal-and-strategic-aspects/*.

81. Giles, "Divided by a Common Language."

82. Timothy L. Thomas, "Dialectical versus Empirical Thinking: Ten Key Elements of the Russian Understanding of Information Operations," *Journal of Slavic Military Studies*, Vol. 11, No. 1, 1998, pp. 40-62.